WHY THE GYM DIDN'T WORK FOR YOU

The Missing Link for Fitness Success

by

MICHELLE DENSMORE, CPT, LCSW

CONTENTS

Dedication

To my wife, Jen, for her unwavering love and support in all that my wild brain can dream up. Thank you for always staying by my side.

To every client that I've had the pleasure of coaching: thank you for motivating me, inspiring me, and teaching me how to push myself more than I ever thought possible.

To my friend and mentor, Pat Rigsby, for telling me to write a book until I finally said yes. I am forever grateful for your guidance.

Introduction

In the decade that I've been in the fitness industry, I've talked with hundreds of people about their desire to lose weight and get fit. I've found that in nearly all cases, a person knows the basics of what they need to do.

They know they should probably eat better, and they know they should probably move their body more. They're right. In a nutshell, those 2 things are what need to happen in order for someone to look and feel better, and become more fit.

The tendency of most people I've heard from was to jump on any spark of motivation, which usually came about around New Year's or perhaps ahead of a high school reunion, wedding, or some other big event. A person purchased a gym membership, committed themselves to a "diet," and went from zero to 150 in 2 days. It never lasted. And, on the other side, the person came out feeling defeated, frustrated, and worse off than when they started.

After hearing this over and over, from scores of people, I started to wonder why.

If they knew what to do, why weren't they successful in doing it? Where was the disconnect between knowing and acting? What was missing?

I turned to my expertise as a licensed therapist and social worker to help me find the answer. What I came to realize was that people were entirely skipping the critical part of Training the Brain to make the exercise and nutrition choices into habits that stuck for more than just a week.

In fact, I left my full-time job at a big box gym to open my own personal training studio because I believed that Training the Brain was so important that it would be the center of my training philosophy.

And this had no room in mainstream, big-box gyms. People were there to sweat, perform a few exercises, and leave. There was no room (both literally and metaphorically) to address a person's habits, stress level, coping mechanisms, or sleep. Trainers were expected to crank out as many training sessions as possible in a day, therefore, making the gym the most money.

I couldn't live with myself as a trainer knowing that I was failing to address most of a more comprehensive equation, and so I created that place on my own.

Six years later, I have developed the only personal training studio that equally focuses on training a person's body and brain--Lucky13Fitness. I have worked with all sorts of people—men, women, teens, business professionals, parents, retirees, and more. All of whom understand that it takes more than just squats, push-ups, and salads to transform a person's life into one that is happy, healthy, and truly fulfilling inside and out. They've been down the typical path and they know it's not a strategy for long-term success. They're tired of the yo-yo, up and down, and they're ready to commit to more than just a "gym membership." They're ready to embark on a unique, transformative experience.

I hope you enjoy this book and a glimpse inside my life and methods.

Enjoy!

--Michelle

1

The Typical Path

At some point you decided that enough was enough. You were sick of your pants fitting too snugly. You were sick of half the shirts in your closet being "15-pounds ago." You'd had it with dreading every family beach trip because you dreaded putting on a bathing suit. And, most of all, you were sick of not being happy with the person you were—inside and out.

So, you decided to take action. You took the first step of your journey. And, somewhere along that journey, to become a more healthy and fit person, you joined a gym. It might have been a $10/month economy gym that you justified joining because it was so cheap. Or, it could have been a super "fancy schmancy" $150+/month club that looked crisp and inviting, and smelled like eucalyptus and success when you walked in. Or, different still, it could have been any other big box gym in between those two price points and offerings.

Regardless, you joined a gym with one thing in mind: feeling and looking better than you did when you started. When you joined, you were full of hope. Hope for the changes that would take place, and hopeful for a body and a life that you'd been dreaming of.

The hope for something better is probably what made it so easy to sign your name on the dotted line and commit to a year (or more) of membership—thereby belonging to the gym and its culture.

The first few weeks were exactly as you pictured. Your gym bag, packed neatly with stylish, new clothes and sneakers, awaited you at the end of a long work day. Though tired, you eagerly grabbed it and headed off for your first gym experience.

The pressure to figure out some of the more complicated machines, or to pick up the dumbbells or Kettlebells without hurting your body or your ego was too much. So, you stuck with what you felt comfortable with, hoping that each bead of sweat was created equal, and that if you were moving, it wouldn't really matter which machines you used.

You dutifully spent an hour or so sweating in any way you could. The treadmill, elliptical, stair climber, resistance machines, and others all became your new friends in the first few weeks of your journey.

At first, you were sore after each workout, but you enjoyed the tangible evidence that you were working hard, and that change would come.

Now fast forward three weeks, or perhaps even a month. Life started getting busy. Packing your gym bag at night to prep for the next morning was no longer an excitement. It had, instead, turned into an annoying or even a dreaded activity.

Going to the gym was one more thing on your seemingly never-ending "to do" list that loomed over you daily.

Making time for the gym amongst work deadlines, family responsibilities, and seasonal activities (summer BBQ's, vacation, or holiday parties/celebrations) became increasingly difficult. The initial excitement you had was wearing off quickly. And, to add even more aggravation, the lack of results made it even harder to stay motivated to show up consistently.

Maybe, you told yourself, if you had lost the 15 or 20 pounds you were hoping to, then you'd have more desire to go. Then, it would be worth it. But all that seemed to be happening was a whole bunch of nothing. Your arms didn't look any more toned, your stomach still wasn't firm and flat, and the thighs you were trying to outrun were still there.

Eventually, the outlook full of ambition that led you to sign up for the gym in the first place turned a bit gloomier. The regular gym schedule that you once had pushed yourself to develop with the best of intentions, became abandoned, and so too did your hope for change.

If only you had known at the time why your dedicated efforts had not been successful. If you had only known the very important reason that you were unable to hit your goals. Then you may have felt a little relief from the overwhelming feeling of failure.

2

Why It Didn't Work

Now that I've made you read and
practically relive the failure of your own
similar gym experience—which probably
made you feel bad for yourself all over
again... I want to say that it wasn't your
fault.

Nope. Not your fault. I've heard this
story time and time again. I can't even
count how many people I've talked to
who dove head first into a fitness journey
doing exactly as I just described. It just
seemed like the right thing to do.
Common sense would say that if you want
to lose weight, you should join a gym and
sweat. Then you'll lose weight, right?
Wrong. As you already know, it rarely
works that way. One of the biggest
reasons why this simple plan goes south
for people is the reliance on the initial
excitement to fuel the whole process. The
day you decided you were going to make a
change, and you walked into that gym to
sign up, you had the highest level of

motivation possible. The anticipation created an excitement that acted as fuel to get you going. And, that's great. But that bit of fuel simply cannot sustain an entire lifetime of being healthy and fit. It just won't work (I know I'm preaching to the choir here.).

Willpower is defined by Dictionary.com as "control of one's impulses and actions; self-control." Merriam-Webster defines willpower as "energetic determination." We all have some level of willpower and it varies from person to person, but more importantly, it varies across periods of time for each of us. Think of willpower like the ocean at the shoreline—it ebbs and flows back and forth, largely dependent on what's happening in the surrounding environment. Willpower can be strong in an environment that is calm and peaceful, but can weaken when one or more stressors enter that environment.

When you first signed up for the gym, your willpower was strong. You had an energetic determination to follow through on your commitment. You promised yourself that you'd do whatever it took to feel and look better. But, because you are human, that level of energetic determination waned with time. Other stressors popped up, as they undoubtedly do in life, and the willpower weakened. The more stressors that were present, in competition with your determination to stick to your gym plan, the weaker the willpower became.

Willpower will never solely be enough for anyone to create long-lasting change. Willpower alone will never allow a person to develop the necessary habits they need not only to achieve their goals, but to sustain them throughout life as well.

Another big reason that the typical path failed you is because there was nothing in place to hold you accountable or to keep you from quitting. When you signed up for your gym membership, they likely took your credit card details so that they could bill you each month, and they gave you a little key tag so you could check in at the front desk during each visit. But what they didn't give you was a phone call if they didn't see you for a week. They didn't come over to you when you were on the elliptical or treadmill and say "C'mon, I know you're tired, but I want to you to give 100% today—make this trip to the gym worth it!" And they definitely didn't schedule a time to talk with you on the phone regularly to check in and answer any questions you might have had.

There was nobody waiting for you to show up 3 times per week, like you had promised yourself you would, at the beginning. There was nobody to assess whether or not you were making any progress toward your goals. And, there was nobody that reached out when you started slipping in your attendance.

In short, there was nobody there for you, in your corner, with your best intentions at heart, helping you stick to your promise and be successful.

Heck, I'm guessing that when you stopped showing up altogether, they just continued to bill your credit card each month. This is what I call "making a donation to the gym." They likely did this until you finally called or showed up to cancel your membership.

Lastly, the typical path failed you because at no point did anyone teach you that it takes more than just 60 minutes on the elliptical twice per week to make true transformation happen. The typical path did not come with a coach to educate and explain that your nutrition and mindset matter about as much as your exercise does and, at the beginning, they matter more. The typical path didn't come with a manual that outlined how to incorporate the right amounts of everything into your life to prevent you from feeling completely overwhelmed.

In my decade as a personal trainer and coach, I have made it my mission to help people who have been let down by the typical path, and who have become jaded toward just about everything fitness related. I have worked with individuals who have tried over and over to reach the goals that they so badly want and so badly deserve—once and for all.

I do so by asking people to trust me to take them down a path less traveled. It's a path that appears less "sexy" and one that certainly requires courage and self-reflection. But, if you have the courage to take this path, you'll find that it will bring true transformation and deep happiness.

In the following chapters, I'm going to take you down that path. I'm going to explain an approach to weight loss, fat loss, and overall fitness that will deliver a

different, and much more satisfying,
outcome than the typical path offered you
before.

3

A Better Approach

Now that you understand *why* the typical path failed you, I am going to share a better approach. This approach is one that removes willpower as being the only driver for success. This approach focuses on the long game, instead of the quick fix. And, this approach will be one that helps you reach your goals, and more importantly, keep the results around long-term.

In order to execute this better approach, the first step is changing your lens from thinking "How can I do this as quickly as possible?" to "I am going to make a long-term lifestyle transformation."

It all starts with making a single change or improvement from where you are now. It cannot all happen at once. Once that first change or improvement becomes a new habit, then it's time to focus on another change or improvement. Small changes or improvements that are built upon consistently will always add up to enormous results.

These changes or improvements are centered around adjusting your behaviors or habits to those which will yield your desired outcomes. For example, eating McDonald's for lunch every day might be the "quick and easy" option that you've chosen for the past few years, but it's not serving your goals. So, the behavior must shift to something that will yield a better outcome, like getting a salad at the salad bar instead.

Unwinding after work by flopping on the couch and watching Netflix for 4 hours, or playing your favorite video game until bedtime will need to shift into going for an evening stroll, or playing a pickup basketball game with friends. The more the new behaviors are incorporated into daily life, the sooner they will feel like the "new normal" and will become habits.

Small steps that I encourage people to start with are things like drinking more water; getting veggies at every single meal; exercising at least 30 minutes per day, at least 3 days per week; and getting 7 hours of sleep each night. Remember, these happen one at a time, not all at once.

The overall key to the better approach lies in taking one step at a time, and being consistent in doing so. It's less "sexy" than the 30 Day Fat Blast Cleanse that you see advertised on TV, but the fruits of your labor will be tenfold.

Theodore Roosevelt once said: "Nothing in the world is worth having or worth doing unless it means effort, pain, difficulty... I have never in my life envied a human being who led an easy life. I have envied a great many people who led difficult lives and led them well."

I am certainly not saying that there's zero enjoyment without suffering, but when it comes to living a life in which you feel and look your best, there's going to be a little work involved. In the next chapter, I'll start to break that work down into steps you can understand and achieve.

4

Developing Healthy
Habits

Developing healthy habits may not sound
much like the most fun or thrilling way to
get skinny fast. That's because—it's not.

Developing healthy habits is exactly the antithesis of what you see blasted at you through the media, trying to get you to impulse buy the latest diet book, powder, pill, or contraption.

You might be someone who not only joined a gym, hoping to lose weight and get fit, but you may have also tried your hand at other, flash-in-the-pan approaches like juice cleanses, the Shake Weight, the vibrating ab belt, creams, pills, etc. These things don't work over the long haul, and if you've tried them, you know this already. If you haven't tried them—don't! I could spend a lot of time talking about these quick-fix approaches, but let me just say this: it is critical for you to actually believe in the concept of the "long haul" and approaching things with a transformative perspective in order for it to work.

There are a handful of behaviors that yield the outcomes you desire. They don't take a rocket scientist to understand, but they do take consistency and determination to get you what you want. This is where most people get lost. They can commit to doing these things for a few days or weeks, but then they lose focus. It is the simple act of repeating these basic behaviors over, and over, and over, and over, and over, and over (you get the hint) for them to become habits. And then they become a bit easier to follow through with. You still may not love doing them, but they happen with a little less frustration and aggravation than before.

This point is so critical that I'm actually going to make the bold statement and say:

If there was ever a "secret key" to fitness success, it would be consistency.

The things you do are actually not complicated or crazy. It's how you do them that makes all the difference.

So, what are these simple behaviors that I want you to incorporate into your life for the rest of your lifetime?

1. **DRINK MORE WATER**

Ditch the soda, Frappuccino, juice, and excessive amounts of coffee. Replace with good old H2O! Add ice, fresh squeezed lemon/lime, or make hot herbal tea. These all count as hydration. I suggest the benchmark of getting one-half of your body weight in ounces of water per day. And, if you sweat a lot, add more. The simple act of drinking enough water will flush so much unwanted crap from your body that you may actually see the scale drop a bit. You will probably also feel your pants fit a bit looser, too.

2. **EAT VEGGIES AT EVERY MEAL**

Yes, eat veggies at *every* meal. Yes, even at breakfast. Throw some spinach or broccoli into your eggs. It may take a bit to get used to, but adding one serving of veggies into a meal can be very easy. You'll learn quickly what you like, and when you do, simply repeat that until you want a change. It's actually nice to put things on autopilot like that. Make it easy for yourself.

3. EXERCISE AT LEAST 30 MINUTES PER DAY, AT LEAST 3 DAYS PER WEEK

You are busy, I know. You have a job, a spouse, kids, a home, a life! You're probably wondering how you're going to fit this in, on top of everything else. Wasn't this the reason you quit the gym in the first place—having no time? Notice I didn't say "go to the gym for 30 minutes per day, 3 days per week."

Exercise can happen anywhere. I suggest starting with a walk. Walk before work, walk on your lunch hour, walk with your spouse and/or kids when you get home.

When you plan a visit with friends, suggest a hike rather than a meal. There are plenty of other options, too.

Love basketball? Join a pick-up league or rec league. Do you love the outdoors? Find a friend who will commit to hiking, biking, canoeing, or running with you regularly. There are a million options to choose from. The key here is to find something you enjoy doing (or at least don't hate doing). If you hate running, please do not read this as instruction to run for 30 minutes per day, 3 days per week. Exercise doesn't have to suck. When you incorporate your interests, and your friends and family, it can be enjoyable. And, when you approach it this way, you're a lot more likely to have it stay in your schedule consistently for the long run.

4. GET AT LEAST 7 HOURS OF SLEEP EACH NIGHT

I have to laugh as I type that one. There was a time in my life, not so long ago, where I would have given my left arm for a 7 hour stretch of sleep. When my son was born, like all moms, I went through a period of sleep deprivation like none other. From nursing every few hours around the clock to waking up in a craze to make sure my newborn was still breathing, sleep eluded me for what felt like an eternity.

But, as a result of this "unofficial research study" I conducted on the effects of sleep deprivation, I realized that all the real science out there is spot on as it relates to this subject. I could get deep into all the reasons that sleep is the key to all things amazing, but I'll sum it up in a few sentences.

Sleep is when your body goes into recovery and repair mode. All the work you do in the gym actually manifests into results if, and when, your body gets enough sleep to do the repair.

Adequate sleep means less stress hormones running through your body, and that leads to less cravings for mile-high nachos and a pint of ice cream at random times of the day or night. The list goes on and on. The bottom line here: get 7 hours of sleep. Scrolling through Facebook or Instagram for the 10th time tonight won't help you get the results you want. So put down the phone and get some shut-eye.

5. FOLLOW THE 80/20 NUTRITION RULE

I love this rule. In short, this rule means that you will never have to say "goodbye" to any food/drink on a permanent basis, ever again. Yes, you read that right. If you love molten chocolate fudge cake, you can eat it. If you dream about a huge slice of New York style pizza, you won't have to live without it.

In addition, the 80/20 rule replaces the evil word that so many people use when they decide to indulge in their favorite treat food. It's the word cheat. I cringe when people use it in this context. I believe that cheating is something you do on your spouse, your taxes, or a test. And if you get caught, you get in trouble. It has a negative connotation. We think of it as something to be ashamed of, and something to hide from others. When we bring these negative associations to a food experience, we likely end up feeling ashamed, mad, or frustrated with ourselves.

With the 80/20 rule, you turn a "cheat" into a "planned treat." The way to use the 80/20 rule is that for 80% of the time, you eat wholesome, unprocessed food to nourish your body. The remaining 20% is left for your favorite food or drink items that fall outside that description; in other words, it's the pizza, cake, or Kahlua mudslide. If you keep consumption of these types of foods to 20% only, you'll be able to maintain good health and fitness. The best part is that you won't feel deprived or forbidden from eating your favorite treats. And you'll never have to "cheat" again.

6. **PRACTICE POSITIVE MESSAGES**

We, especially women, have a hard time saying anything nice about ourselves. We are much quicker to criticize our "thunder thighs" than we are to appreciate our beautiful complexion. We have no trouble picking apart all the things that are wrong with us; things not good enough, not big enough, not small enough, or things that we haven't achieved yet.

We rarely, if ever, take a moment to say something positive to ourselves about ourselves. So, start by telling yourself one positive thing each day. Set a time each day to do it, like when you are in front of the mirror getting ready. Say it out loud. Look yourself in the eye. And try, with all of your might, to actually believe it.

Yeah, it may feel a bit corny, but that's only because you're not used to saying nice things to yourself. Positive messages can be about your physical traits, personality, mentality, or any other part of you.

Eventually, you'll believe these messages, and know them to be true. You'll build confidence in who you are as a person and grow your self-worth, and that goes a long way when it comes to becoming the happiest, best version of you.

And, that's it. Those 6 key things put into practice daily will be a game changer. The key is to develop each of them into habits that become part of your daily routine. A behavior becomes a habit with repetition. Lots of practice will be needed before these become second nature. So, work on one of them at a time. Taking on all 6 at once would be too overwhelming and you'd end up doing them all for a few weeks, and then give them all up.

Pick one to start with. Which one? Your choice entirely. My suggestion is that you pick one that seems "not so bad." Do not start with the one that seems most difficult. Once you make the first one a habit, you'll have improved your overall physical wellbeing, but you'll also have a nice confidence boost as well.

In the next chapter, I will discuss training the one part of your body that you've probably never realized needed its own training routine: your brain. The brain is the boss, and it gives out the commands to the rest of the body. So, if we want success with the biceps, glutes, and abs, the brain must be on board. Get ready to practice sets and reps of a different kind: habit-based training for your brain.

5

Training the Brain

A behavior that is not yet a habit requires
an external cue to initiate the behavior.
You cannot simply "try to remember" or
use willpower. For example, if you are
working at improving your hydration,

you'll need some sort of reminder to sip water every so often.

Just because you become conscious of the fact that you need to drink more water, and you know that being more hydrated will help your overall health, doesn't mean that you'll all of a sudden go from 8 ounces per day to 80 ounces per day.

You need an external cue to remind you. Something that isn't your own self trying to remember on its own. Try using Post-It notes, an alarm on a smartphone, written reminders, or a private coach. These are all external cues that can help remind you to initiate the behavior.

Many of my clients have had success with setting alarms on their iPhones to go off every 30 to 60 minutes as a reminder to drink water. Yes, it may seem that an alarm going off every hour would be disruptive and annoying, but it's all worth it in the end.

The behavior (let's stick with the hydration example) must be repeated many times before the external cue is no longer needed. For many people, it takes about 3 weeks, but for some it can be longer or shorter. If you choose to use the smartphone alarm, you'll know it's becoming a habit when you sip water and preemptively shut off the alarm so you don't have to hear it.

This is what I have coined as "Training The Brain." Just like we do bicep curls to train our biceps, and squats to train our legs and glutes, we repeat behaviors over and over to train our brains. And training your brain to develop healthy habits is what will set you up for success. Remember, just as one bicep curl won't give you "guns." one act of Training the Brain won't create a habit. Repetition and time are key elements both for training the physical body and the mental muscle.

I can't stress enough that you should focus on one behavior at a time. It's best to put all of your efforts in one place to make entirely certain that it becomes as ingrained into your daily routine as brushing your teeth. When that behavior feels like second nature, it has become a habit. Then, and only then, should you shift your focus on adding a second behavior.

These new habits must fit within your lifestyle construct. They must be sustainable for you in the long term in order for this all to work. Once again, I'll bring up the running example: if you really dislike (or hate) running, but you try to make it a habit by doing it 3 days per week, you can pretty much be certain that you will not stick with it long term. The habits must mesh with you and your

lifestyle. Sure, you may never love eating
a veggie with your breakfast, and that will
be just something you tolerate, but on the
whole you should make this as
comfortable an experience as possible.
Remember, this is the plan you're setting
into place for the rest of your life, so you
better tolerate it, at worst, and learn to
love it, at best.

I often frame this to my clients in the
following way: you may never love eating
spinach, but you'll love the result of
eating spinach. Eating spinach for a week
will give you the result you want... but
only for a week. Getting results that last a
week or two is easy. Almost any fitness or
nutrition program/diet on the market can

do that. It's keeping the results that's the bigger challenge. The key is to keep eating spinach so you can keep enjoying the fruits of your labor. In the next chapter, I'll discuss long term results and how to attain them.

6

Long Term Results

I've used the words "long term" and "lifestyle" several times throughout this book. And I've done so on purpose. I've done so because, if you haven't gotten the gist already, developing a healthy lifestyle that persists and stays strong in the face of stress and adversity is the only way you'll keep the body and life you've been trying forever to achieve.

Developing a "healthy lifestyle" means you'll develop a sense of balance, and you'll know when you can enjoy your 20% and when you need to stay focused on the 80%. You'll probably be one of those people who does so with such seeming ease that you'll have other people ask you how you do it.

Because the habits you learn will be learned slowly and over time, the likelihood that they will stick for the long run is *much* higher than trying to change everything all at once. And it is certainly more successful than trying to shock your system with an unsafe grapefruit juice and cayenne pepper cleanse.

When healthy habits are in place, you are best positioned to keep making progress. Even when life throws you a curveball and you get temporarily sidetracked, you won't just fall off the wagon never to return again. You'll be able to recognize and correct your actions, and get right back on track in a few days. Your hard work developing a group of healthy habits that make up your healthy lifestyle will pay off (and pay dividends) over the long run.

And, having been in the fitness industry over a decade, the number 1 reason (by far) I hear from people as to why they haven't achieved their goals is something like, "Well, I was on a good path, but I got busy and life took over. Before I knew it, I gained all 10 pounds back and then I gained 5 more."

It happens all the time. People try to join a gym and be consistent. They have the best of intentions, just like I discussed back in Chapter One. But, without understanding the power of Training the Brain, they will run into the same pitfalls over and over again.

But, with the approach I am teaching you in this book, you'll know how to avoid these pitfalls and make a plan that will deliver success and satisfaction.

Follow the steps I outlined here, and you won't ever have to tolerate the yo-yo, back and forth, up and down rollercoaster ride of weight loss and weight gain ever again.

7

How to Get Started Today

My hope is that now that you've read this book, you only have one question remaining...How do I get started?

So, in this chapter, I will outline the steps you need to take in order to execute the better approach and leave your days of the typical path behind.

Step 1: DEVELOP A CLEAR GOAL & WHY

Your goal must be crystal clear. It must be specific and it must be measurable. It must have a time constraint. And, it must be realistic for you, given your life.

Your goal cannot be "I want to lose weight." Or, "I want to be more fit." You can start there, but then I want to know what that looks like for you? What does "be more fit" mean? The ability to run a 5K? To run a 5K in 20 minutes? The ability to squat your body weight? The ability to do a plank? You get my point.

When you think you've identified a clear goal, then you'll want to do the most important work of all: developing your "why factor." The why factor is a term I coined when coaching my clients. It is the reason behind achieving the goal in the first place.

To develop your why factor, start by asking yourself this series of questions (I suggest writing or typing your responses):

- What is driving me to reach this goal?
- What will achieving this goal do for me?
- How will I feel when I achieve this goal?
- How will I feel if I don't achieve this goal?

If you're doing this exercise correctly, this will elicit some very personal and emotional answers. This takes the "I want to lose 20 pounds" goal and evolves it into "I want to feel like I did in college, because it was the time where I felt most confident. I was at the head of my class and I was proud of my hard work. I had lots of friends and I felt like I was really on a path to success. I felt like my best self, inside and out. I want to be that confident again, and I want to be proud of myself again. I need to do this so that I can set an example for my daughters. I want them to see their mom as a strong female role model that they can look up to."

Pretty different from "I'd like to lose 20 pounds." Right?

The reason the why factor is so powerful is because each and every one of us has a different one. It personalizes our efforts, and it reminds us of how important the goal is. It serves as a source of motivation and as a fire under your a$$ when you're tired and feeling lazy and don't want to cook a healthy meal or go to the gym.

It can be easy to talk your way out of those things when it's just for "losing 20 pounds," but when you remind yourself of setting a good example for your daughters and regaining pride and confidence in yourself, it can give you the metaphorical kick you need to get going.

Once you have a good, solid why factor, I want you to read it over and then ask yourself "why" one more time. Why do you want the goal? Why do you want to put forth such efforts?

Once you've asked yourself "why?" about 10 times, you've likely got a solid why factor.

Write it down and put it in a place where you'll see it often. You'll need the reminders very frequently, especially at the beginning.

Step 2: IDENTIFY THE TOP 3 BEHAVIORS THAT WILL HELP LEAD YOU TO THE GOAL

I discussed my top five in Chapter 4, and your top three will likely be some of those same five, or versions thereof. My suggestion is that you choose one behavior that addresses your physical body, or fitness level. Choose a second behavior that addresses your nutrition, or relationship with food. And, choose a third behavior that addresses your mindset, or mental/emotional health.

An example of this is:

- Behavior A is committing to walk 30 minutes per day, 3 days per week.
- Behavior B is eating a single serving of veggies at each meal.
- Behavior C is signing up for an email newsletter that sends daily affirmations, and reading the affirmation each day.

Remember, the behaviors need to fit into the construct of your life and must be doable without too many obstacles. For example, you cannot commit to snowshoeing for 30 minutes 3 days per week if you live in Florida. It's just not gonna happen!

Step 3: PICK 1 OF THE 3 AND START TO BUILD IT INTO A HABIT THAT FITS INTO YOUR LIFE

This usually involves creating 1-3 "checklist items" that will guide you on a daily or weekly basis. The checklist is an external reminder to help keep you on track and focused on exactly what you need to do.

For example, if my first focus is to eat a serving of veggies at each meal, my checklist items would be:

- Go food shopping on Sunday mornings and Wednesday after work to buy veggies.
- Wash/peel/chop veggies into ready-to-eat portions.
- Put each portion into a container, so they're ready to use for cooking or to bring to work.

Using this checklist is critical, in my opinion, and helps accomplish a few key things.

First, it helps break down a huge goal into bite-sized chunks that don't feel overwhelming or scary. The bite-sized chunks are things that can be handled, even on a busy day. Second, the checklist provides an honest "did you do it or not" way to hold yourself accountable. You literally either check the box, or not. There's no talking your way out of it. Simple and effective.

With these 3 simple steps, you can say goodbye forever to the typical path and follow a better approach of developing healthy habits, training your brain, and achieving long term results.

When you set out on your journey to lose weight and become more fit, you took the typical path because you didn't know anything else existed. Now, after learning my Train your Brain method, you know how to use habit-based change. And you're ready to make changes that will last for decades to come.

Next Steps

Create Your Plan of Action

In order to achieve the goals that seem big and, at times, hard to achieve, your plan of action will be to work backwards and reverse engineer a plan for success.

1. Set your top 1-3 annual goals. Ex. lose 30 lbs.

2. Set goals for the next quarter (3 months): Ex. lose 10 lbs.

3. Set goals for the next month: Ex. lose 3-4 lbs.

4. Set action steps for each week of the month that will bring you closer to your goals: Ex: meal prep 3 meals per week, strength train 3 times per week, get 7-8 hours of sleep nightly.

5. Set action steps for THIS week: go to grocery store and purchase food for 3 meals this week; block out 3 hours in my schedule for strength training this week; shut off all electronics by 9:30pm for a 10pm bedtime.

6. Set action steps for each day: Ex. Today, I will make meatballs with zucchini noodles and put meal into Tupperware for lunch tomorrow; leave work by 5pm to make it to 5:30 training session; finish all computer work by 9pm, and finish all electronics by 9:30pm.

This may initially feel a little laborious, but it most definitely helps take a big goal like "lose 30 pounds" (which can leave you feeling like you don't know where to begin) and break it into "bite-sized" chunks that you can achieve each day.

Those bite-sized chunks are the behaviors that will, over time, become habits.

Those habits, done with consistency, will result in the 30 pounds of weight loss.

Focus on filling your day-to-day with key habits, and the long run will take care of itself.

A Free Gift for You

As a special gift to you for reading this book, please visit the link below for your FREE copy of my Create Your Plan of Action spreadsheet and my "Ultimate Guide to Diet and Fat Loss."

Visit here:
www.lucky13fitness.com/book-bonus-material

Author Bio

Michelle Densmore, CPT, LCSW is a
nationally recognized personal trainer
who draws on her extensive training to
motivate and inspire each of her
clients toward meeting goals in all areas
of life. She believes that "Your body can
do it if you put your mind to it." And also
that habit-based behavior change is the
key to success.

Michelle believes that the Mental Muscle is important and strongly believes in "Training the Brain!"

In addition to writing for the Lucky13Ftitness Blog, Michelle has been featured as a guest blogger for Runner's World, Zelle, and LoziLu Mud Runs.

She's also been a featured guest speaker at health and fitness expos and workshops. When she is not working, Michelle enjoys training for and competing in road races and triathlons. She also loves to travel with her wife, son, and their 2 Rhodesian Ridgebacks.

Connect with Michelle:

Email: michelle@lucky13fitness.com

Facebook:
https://www.facebook.com/Lucky13Fitness/

Twitter: https://twitter.com/Lucky13Fit

YouTube:
https://www.youtube.com/user/lucky13fit